Cool Cats

By Beth Adelman

The
Child's
World®
www.childsworld.com

Published in the United States of America by The Child's World®
1980 Lookout Drive • Mankato, MN 56003-1705
800-599-READ • www.childsworld.com

ACKNOWLEDGMENTS

The Child's World®: Mary Berendes, Publishing Director

Produced by Shoreline Publishing Group LLC
President / Editorial Director: James Buckley, Jr.
Designer: Tom Carling, carlingdesign.com
Cover Design: Slimfilms

Photo Credits
Cover–Tammy Rao
Interior–All photos by Tammy Rao except: Dreamstime.com: 6, 15,
17 (2), 18, 21, 24, 26 bottom; iStock: 26 top.

LIBRARY OF CONGRESS CATALOG-IN-PUBLICATION DATA

Adelman, Beth.
  Cool cats / by Beth Adelman.
    p. cm. — (Reading rocks!)
  Includes index.
  ISBN-13: 978-1-59296-865-7 (library bound : alk. paper)
  ISBN-10: 1-59296-865-1 (library bound : alk. paper)
  1. Cats—Juvenile literature. I. Title. II. Series.

SF445.7.A34 2007
636.8—dc22

2007004191

CONTENTS

WHAT CATS
need

Cats can be beautiful and graceful or silly and sweet. They like to sleep in the sun and run up the back of the couch. They wake us up in the morning and wait for us to come home in the evening—all because they love to be with us!

Some people think cats are independent, but that's really not true. Cats need us, and they love to do things with us. They love to snuggle up and sleep next to us. They also love to play with us.

Is your cat your best friend? Does she always keep your secrets? Does she hang out with you? Let's learn more about cats and how you can help them live good lives—with you!

See those pointy ears? Because cats' hearing is so good, loud noises are extra loud to them. If you play your stereo or TV really loud, your cat probably won't want to stick around.

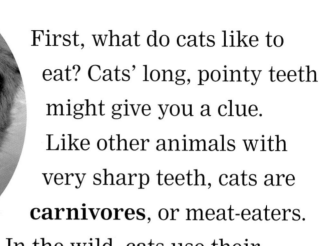

See those sharp, pointy teeth? They help cats catch and eat prey.

First, what do cats like to eat? Cats' long, pointy teeth might give you a clue. Like other animals with very sharp teeth, cats are **carnivores**, or meat-eaters. In the wild, cats use their pointed teeth to catch **prey** such as mice and birds.

Want to have dinner with your cat? You don't have to catch a mouse! Some people like to feed their cats the same foods that people eat, such as cooked meat and fish. Many cats also like **dairy** foods, such as milk and cottage cheese. It's OK to feed your cat a little bit of these foods. But be careful! Too much "people food" can make your cat sick.

You should never feed your cat onions, garlic, spicy foods, or sweets—especially chocolate. These foods can make your cat very, very sick.

Older cats and kittens each have special needs. Choose food that fits your cat's age.

Cats sleep about 18 hours a day. Of course, that means they are awake just six hours a day. They usually spend two or three of those hours **grooming** themselves—licking and licking all over.

With all that grooming, you might think they don't need any help from you. But they do. That's because

Family Cat Care

Make a list of all the things your cat needs every day and what times they should be done. Then your family can get together and decide who will take on each job. Everyone will know what they are supposed to do and when . . . and your cat will know she can count on you.

Here are
some types of
brushes you
can use
to groom
your cat.

cats swallow the hair they pull from their coat. If they swallow too much hair, it can make them throw up. You can help your cat by grooming it with a special cat brush. The brush gets rid of the hair before your cat can swallow it.

Cats lick their paws and then rub their paws on their fur to groom themselves.

If your cat has short hair, you'll need to brush her once a week. If she has long hair, she probably needs to be brushed every day.

9

Even though cats love to be with us, they also like to be alone. Just like you, cats want to be left alone when they're eating and when they're sleeping. And just like you, they don't want to be bothered when they're going to the bathroom.

Cats also like to have someplace secret to hide—maybe a paper bag or a box or a little tent—when they're feeling worried.

This cat is peering out from beneath a chair—a good hiding place for a cautious cat.

Cats like to have someplace high up where they can sit and watch things, too. Maybe that's the top of a bookshelf or a tall **cat tree**. When kitty is sitting in the highest spot in a room, she can see everything that's going on.

From up on a window ledge, this cat can keep an eye on everything going on below.

Another place cats go is their litter box—that's where they go to the bathroom. Make sure your cat's litter box is always clean.

Your cat should visit a **veterinarian** at least once a year for a checkup. The vet will listen to your cat's heart and check her breathing. The vet will also look at your cat's teeth to make sure they're clean. She will look in your cat's eyes and ears. The vet will feel your

A trip to the veterinarian each year will help keep your cat in good health.

This vet is checking a cat's teeth, lips, and gums to make sure they're healthy.

Getting Her Shots

The vet may give your cat a shot to keep her from getting sick. Not all cats need such shots every year. Your veterinarian will help your family decide what your cat needs.

cat all over to see if she has any lumps or bumps on her skin.

Watch for these signs that your cat might not be feeling well:

- Your cat suddenly stops eating.
- Your cat throws up a lot.
- She starts to limp.
- She starts to cry a lot or acts differently than she normally does.

If you notice any of these things, bring your cat to the vet right away. Your pet is counting on you!

JUST BEING A Cat

Cats have very keen senses. They can hear sounds that are too quiet for people to hear. In the wild, cats depend on this great hearing to listen for prey. Their pointy ears help them tell which direction a sound is coming from.

Cats can also smell things that people can't. Like their keen hearing, cats' great sense of smell helps them find prey. Cats can even recognize people and other cats by the smells they give off.

Cats don't need very much light to see. They can find their way in very dark rooms or on really dark nights. Cats also get help from their whiskers to find their way. A cat's whiskers let it feel when items are very close by.

Cats' eyes glow because they have a special part inside that reflects light.

This cat is feeling very good about herself right now. You can tell by the raised tail.

Cats communicate by moving different parts of their bodies. You can tell a lot about a cat's mood by watching its ears and tail. When both are held straight up, the cat is feeling relaxed and bold. When both are held out, she's feeling cautious. When a cat's ears are flat and her tail is down, she's ready for a fight.

Tasting a Smell

Have you ever seen your cat sniff something and then make a funny face? It's really "tasting" what it's smelling. Cats use their tongues to sweep smells into their mouths. Then a special organ in the roof of their mouths tells them what different scents are.

Cats also send "scent letters" to other cats. They have special scent **glands** on the sides of their faces and the bottoms of their paws. These glands leave smells that people can't notice—but other cats can! These smells say things like, "I was here," or "This is the chair I like to sit on."

This cat's head and tail are down; she's feeling a little nervous.

Cats are so graceful when they move, they sometimes look as if they're dancing. Their bodies are specially made to make them slinky and light on their feet.

The bones in a cat's back have thick cushions between them. This means kitty can curl up and make herself shorter or stretch out and make

With a big push from its strong thigh muscles, this cat leaps!

herself longer. This comes in handy when jumping onto things.

A cat's powerful thighs are also handy jumping tools. If you had thighs like a cat, they'd each be as big around as your waist and you could jump to the top of a house!

Cats are very flexible. They can curl up in ways that other animals can't.

Cats also use their nails to grab and hold things, as this cat is going to do to this toy.

Does your cat scratch the back of your couch or your mattress? You may think she's being naughty. Really, she's just being a cat. Cats scratch because they need to. Scratching helps cats keep their nails healthy. Scratching pulls the old covers off their nails so the new nail underneath can grow. You might see the old nail covers on the floor after your cat has finished scratching. These old nail covers look like tiny **crescent** moons.

Cats also scratch to get a good stretch. They sink their claws into something above their heads, then pull down. They stretch all the way from their neck to their rumps. Cats love to scratch things that are tall and sturdy!

This closeup shows a cat's curved claws. These nail covers sometimes fall off when a cat scratches.

If you give your kitty a tall, sturdy post to scratch on, she'll leave your furniture alone.

TIME TO
Play

Cats who stay indoors live twice as long as cats who wander around outside. But when cats stay inside all the time, it's easy for them to get bored. That's why you need to take time to play with your cat.

Sure, you can leave cat toys on the floor or hanging from doorknobs. But these things don't move around in exciting ways. Only you can make kitty's toys interesting for her. Only you can play games with her and teach her tricks.

Cats like to play, but sometimes they just want to snuggle up with us.

Cats Love Catnip

Catnip is a plant that's in the same family as mint. It's easy to grow, and cats love it! Take a few catnip leaves and crumble them up on top of your cat's favorite toy. Watch her sniff and rub the toy. She won't want to leave it alone!

Cats love to wait and watch while they're playing. To them, it's like being back in the wild.

For cats, playing is like hunting. So imagine kitty is chasing a mouse around the house. What would the mouse do? It would run away, of course! It might run under the couch or behind a chair leg. Making toys move like this is more fun for your cat.

But cats don't always chase their prey. Sometimes they watch it carefully and wait for it to stand still. That's because resting prey is easier to catch than running prey. Cats plan for just the right moment to **pounce**, and then . . . *whump*! They catch it! Try to move toys in a stop-and-go pattern. Cats love it!

Move your cat's toy under, around, and behind things. Your cat might chase the toy, or she might watch carefully. When she does pounce, make sure you let her catch the toy. What a great hunter!

This cat is stalking another kind of mouse . . . get it?

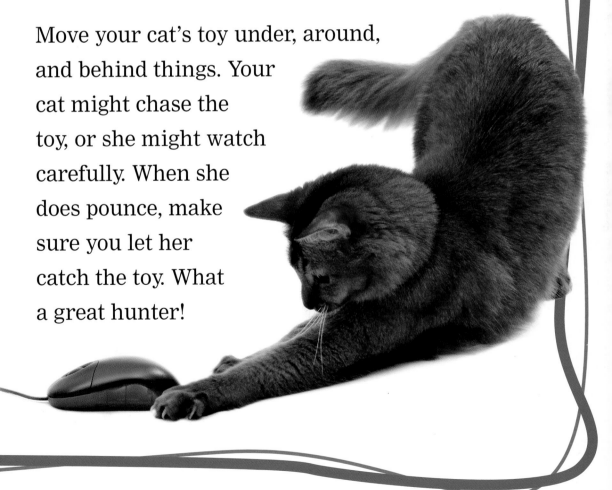

Wild kinds of cats live all over the world. Some are the size of house cats. Others are big, such as lions and tigers. They hunt different prey, depending on where they live. So some cats hunt mice. Others hunt birds. Some cats even hunt wiggly bugs.

Lynx live in North America, Europe, and Asia.

Pet cats like to play with toys that look or move like the prey their wild relatives hunt. Some cats like feathery toys. Other cats like little squeaky toys that wiggle under things. You can also find balls that roll along the floor or big soft toys that your cat can carry around.

Not every kid likes to play ball or build things, and not every cat likes to play with the same toys. Watch carefully to see what kinds of toys and games get your cat excited.

The movement of this feather on a stick is what attracts the cats.

Here are three fun games to play with your cat.

1. Put a small treat in a paper cup and place it on the floor. Kitty will have to either pull the treat out of the cup with her paw, or knock over the cup. If she has trouble, help her find the treat. Be patient!

2. Open a magazine or a newspaper to make a tent on the floor. Make a cat toy poke out from under the tent, then "sneak" back in. To your cat, the toy looks like a mouse darting in and out of a hiding place.

3. Throw an old towel over a low table. Watch how fast kitty gets under this "tent." In fact, just being

in the tent is exciting to a cat. But the game gets even better when you wiggle a cat toy just under the edge of the towel (a feather works really well, too). You can also wiggle your fingers along the towel's edge. Your cat will love this game!

Cats need lots of love. And they have lots of love to give in return. That's what makes cats the "purr-fect" pet!

Whew! After all that playing, it's time to relax for a few minutes!

GLOSSARY

carnivores   animals that eat meat

cat tree   a special piece of furniture with several shelves on it that cats can climb

crescent   a curved figure with two points, like the shape of a new moon

dairy   foods made from milk

glands   organs in the body that produce something, such as saliva, sweat, or special smells

grooming   keeping hair neat and clean by brushing (or licking)

pounce   to jump on top of something and grab it

prey   animals that are food for other animals

veterinarian   a doctor who takes care of animals

FIND OUT MORE

BOOKS

Eyewitness Cat
by Juliet Clutton-Brock (DK Publishing, 2004)
Learn how cats communicate, why cats play with prey, why they eat grass, and much more in this fact-packed book.

Totally Fun Things to Do With Your Cat
by Maxine Rock (Jossey-Bass, 1998)
Discover great games using everyday objects such as paper bags, balls, and string, or teach your cat to do tricks. Basic training tips are also included, along with fascinating facts about cats.

What Your Cat Needs
by Liz Palika (DK Publishing, 2000)
This book contains advice for cat owners, illustrated with plenty of photographs and charts. You'll find information about the equipment your cat needs, diet, training, grooming, and health.

WEB SITES

Visit our Web page for lots of links about cats and cat care:
www.childsworld.com/links

Note to Parents, Teachers, and Librarians: We routinely check our Web links to make sure they're safe, active sites—so encourage your readers to check them out!

INDEX

BETH ADELMAN is a Certified Cat Behavior Consultant and writes "The Cat Lady" column for the *New York Post* newspaper. She is also the former editor of *Cats* magazine and the author of the award-winning book *Every Cat's Survival Guide to Living With a Neurotic Owner*. She lives with three brilliant and beautiful cats who teach her new things every day.